Lifelines

A play

Amy Rosenthal

Samuel French—London
New York-Toronto-Hollywood

Please see page iv for further copyright information

LIFELINES

First presented at the Royal Court Theatre Upstairs at the Ambassador's Theatre from 28th October to 16th November 1996, with the following cast:

Annie Nina Conti
Robert Silas Carson

Director Indhu Rubasingham

Recorded as an audio-play

LIFELINES

Annie
Robert

The action of the play takes place in Annie's bedroom and Robert's kitchen

Time — The present

LIFELINES

SCENE 1

With as few pieces of furniture as possible, the stage is split to represent Annie's bedroom and Robert's kitchen

Stage left, Annie sits cross-legged on her bed. In front of her is a telephone, a box of tissues, three empty packets of cigarettes, an ashtray and a nail file

Stage right, Robert is perched on the edge of his kitchen table, which holds an uneaten bowl of corn flakes, three empty packets of cigarettes, an ashtray and a telephone

As the Lights come up, Annie is filing her nails. She has been crying heavily and still gives the occasional sob or sniff. Robert is pressing numbers into his telephone

Annie's phone rings sharply

Annie Bastard.

She drops her nail file and blows her nose. As she lifts the receiver, she starts to bite her newly-filed nails

Hallo.
Robert Sarah, darling, I'm sorry. I'm truly sorry. I mean it.
Annie Um, I'm sorry ——
Robert *No*, darling. *I'm* sorry. Please. Let me be sorry ——
Annie No, hold it, shut up. You've got the wrong number.

Robert Who's that?
Annie Well, it's not Sarah.
Robert Well where is she?
Annie How the hell should I know? *Who* is she?
Robert Look, is that 0181 598 9098?
Annie No.
Robert Shit. I really needed to speak to Sarah.
Annie Well *ring* Sarah, for Christ's sake.

A pause. Both bite their nails

Robert Right. Yes. I'll do that. Sorry. Sorry to disturb you.
Annie No problem. Goodbye.
Robert Wait!
Annie (*wearily*) Yes?
Robert Are you — all right?

Pause

Annie Are you a dodgy phone-call?
Robert It's just — you sound …
Annie Go on. Surprise me. You know what colour my knickers
    are. I've had calls like this before, you know.
Robert You sound as though you are in some sort of anguish.
Annie (*softly*) Anguish? That's a strong word.
Robert What did you say your name was?
Annie I said it wasn't Sarah.
Robert Oh, Sarah's my girlfriend. I was trying to call her. I wanted
    to apologize.
Annie So I gathered.
Robert I upset her last night. A lot.
Annie (*mocking*) Was she in anguish?
Robert She — no. Not anguish. But considerable pain.
Annie And how do you differentiate anguish and considerable
    pain?
Robert Anguish is considerably more painful.
Annie Of course. (*Tearful*) I should know.

Robert Sorry. I'm sorry. I'm upsetting you even more. Sarah says I never know when to stop.

Annie Sarah's bloody right.

Robert Sorry.

Annie (*softer*) That's all right. It's all right.

Robert Can I ask you a question?

Annie I can't guarantee an answer.

Robert Is it a man?

Annie Can I ask you a question? Who *are* you?

Robert I'm Robert.

Annie Right.

Robert Hallo.

Annie Hi.

Robert It's just there's a tiredness in your voice which I recognize, you see. It reminds me of ——

Annie Surely not Sarah?

Robert And my mother. And my Aunt Sadie. She married a complete arse. Her rice-pudding tasted of tears.

Annie Look, Richard. All women are not the same. I'm not Sarah and I'm not your mother and I'm certainly not your Aunt Sadie.

Robert Robert.

Annie Pardon?

Robert Well, I know you're not Aunt Sadie. She's in Penge. But if you won't tell me who you *are* …

Annie My name is Annie. Happy now?

Robert Like *Annie Hall.*

Annie Like Annie Hall in that we share the name Annie. But I'm not Annie Hall. And he's not Woody bloody Allen.

Robert Aha, it *is* a man.

Annie Good work, Sherlock.

Robert A lover?

Annie Supposedly. (*She breaks down and grabs for a tissue*) Oh, sod it!

Robert Sarah says I make her feel lonely. Even when we're together.

Annie He makes me feel alone. Totally alone. *Especially* when we're together. When I *am* alone, I feel terrific.

Robert Did you tell him?

Annie I could never tell him that.

Robert No. I could never tell Sarah how she makes me feel sometimes. Kind of — dull and inadequate. Big. Clumsy. I spill things. She notices buttons coming off before they come off.

Annie Oh God, all the effort, the sheer *effort*! And why? He wouldn't *notice* if I stopped brushing my hair. Or my teeth. Or shaving my legs. If I grew a bloody *beard*.

Robert Sarah noticed when I grew a beard.

Annie Or horns! Or scales! Or wings!

Robert But she didn't when I shaved it off ...

Annie Or webbed fucking feet.

Pause

Robert You get used to how someone looks.

Annie Is Sarah pretty?

Robert She's got the loveliest eyes. When she's happy, and they just light up ... last week, when it snowed, I was in town and I saw her — she didn't see me. She was coming out of Boots with Paula, her friend Paula, and she was wearing a red scarf. Bright red. She was laughing and she looked so happy. She looked absolutely gorgeous.

Annie If you love someone, you love them happy *and* sad.

Robert But — when I see those eyes filling up and bubbling over with tears — *again* ...

Annie (*heavily*) So you mop them up. *Again*. That's what you do. Because you care. *If* you care. You should care, Robert. No matter how many times.

Robert I just want her to be happy. I don't know how to make her happy and then keep her happy.

Annie How is it that we can have the same car, the same guitar, the same hat, the same mug, for years, and we're content — but the same person in our lives for just so long, and we stop seeing them when we look at them. We just see cause and effect.

Robert It seems like she's fine for a while and then all of a sudden she's crying her eyes out again, and I don't know what I've done. But I know it's me.

Annie I make up reasons. So I don't have to confront him with everything he fails to do and say. I pretend it's hormonal or seasonal, or a shortage of Vitamin B6.

Robert But how can he know, then? How can he *fail* to fail you if you don't tell him? How can he ever make you happy?

Annie I write him letters, in my head. All the time.

Robert Well what use is that? (*Thoughtfully*) Sarah has a shortage of Vitamin B6.

Annie In my head I leave him. Fifty, sixty times a day.

Robert Why don't you do it?

Annie That's what everyone says. All my friends.

Robert Sarah talks to her friends about me. I know she does. I see it in their faces when they look at me. They know everything about me — they know things *I* don't know. Horrid habits of mine that she's noticed. Personal things. Vital statistics of things. *My* things. Things that are none of their bloody business. Sometimes I can't meet their eyes.

Annie I try to keep it pretty much to myself. But my friends know if I'm unhappy. (*Laughs*) *Anguished*.

Robert But if you *are* so unhappy, Annie …

Annie Robert, do you love Sarah?

Robert Yes. Yes, I see.

Annie But that's not the only reason. There's another reason why I stay with him. A worse reason.

Robert I'd miss her too much. I'd miss her eyes, even full of sodding tears. I'd miss all the lumps of henna mud crap she leaves all over the bathroom, staining everything orange. And the way she recites T.S. Eliot in traffic jams: *The Love Song of J. Alfred Prufrock* in a ten-mile tailback on the Finchley Road. I'd miss the way she watches herself in restaurant mirrors when I'm trying to talk to her.

Annie I do that. Maybe I am like Sarah after all. Did Aunt Sadie do that too?

Robert What's the reason then, Annie? The worse reason?

Annie Oh. Why I don't leave David?

Robert Yes.

Annie (*simply*) Because he'd let me.

Robert What?

Annie Oh, he'd be sorry, he'd be sad. He'd be a very lonely, very lost and lonely man. But he wouldn't stop me. He wouldn't fight. He'd let me go.

Robert Then he doesn't deserve you.

Annie I'm not so great myself.

Robert I think you're a nice girl, Annie.

Annie I think you should ring Sarah. She's waiting.

Pause

Robert Will you be all right?

Annie Tell her all the things you told me. Her lovely eyes. Tell her about the red scarf.

Robert Annie. Will you be all right, Annie Hall?

Annie Yes. One day I will be so bloody fine. I promise.

Robert I've enjoyed talking to you.

Annie Yes. Me too.

Robert And don't let him — oh, look, I'll shut up. Sarah says I don't know when to stop. I'll stop now. I'll let you go. 'Bye Annie.

Robert puts the phone down and the Lights fade at his side of the stage

Annie stays where she is, still holding on to the phone

As the Lights dim on her bedroom ——

Annie Yes, let me go. Lightly. Easily. Don't try to stop me. Just let me go.

SCENE 2

The same, six months later

General Lights up

Annie is in bed, wearing a black lacy nightgown and glasses. She is reading a novel. There are two wineglasses and an empty bottle by the bed, and the space beside Annie looks slept-in. Lazily, she plays with a cigarette

Robert is sitting at the kitchen table, which is littered with bowls, mugs, papers, general mess. Nervously, he grinds out a cigarette. He dials a number on the phone

Annie's phone rings

Annie (*picking up the phone*) Hallo.
Robert God!
Annie I wondered when He was going to get in touch again.
Robert My *God*.
Annie One day a burning bush, next day a BT Chargecard.
Robert I will never laugh at psychological claptrap again, I swear. I will change my ways. I will have my aura polished. I will eat wheatgerm.
Annie You know, I recognize the voice, but the words are going straight past me.
Robert You sound different. More relaxed.
Annie I'm lying down. (*She sits up*) Different from *what*?
Robert I rang you, about six months ago. By mistake. Robert. You remember? You were upset. We talked. I ——
Annie Ah — someone's boyfriend. Sarah. Sarah's boyfriend.
Robert Ex.
Annie Really? I'm sorry.
Robert I'm not. I mean, I am. But I've thought about you a lot, Annie Hall. How's your Woody Allen?
Annie (*softly*) He's — fine. Really fine.

Robert Really? Things are good?
Annie Yes. Things are — good.

A pause. Both light a cigarette

Robert Good.
Annie So how did you happen to call the same wrong number twice in half a year?
Robert You won't believe me if I tell you.
Annie I believe in miracles. I eat wheatgerm.
Robert Do you believe in hypnosis?
Annie Do I believe in hypnosis? Sure I believe in hypnosis! I went to a hypnotist in Harley Street last summer. To give up smoking.
Robert Did it work?
Annie (*glancing at her cigarette*) Why do you ask?
Robert I'm interested to know if it worked.
Annie I mean, why do you ask if I believe in ——
Robert Because I've just been hypnotized to remember the wrong number I dialled six months ago.

A pause. Annie stubs out her cigarette

Annie Why?
Robert I wanted to talk to you again, Annie. I've thought about you a lot. I've wondered how you were.
Annie I'm fine.
Robert You've got a nice voice.
Annie Thank you.
Robert Do you sing? I bet you sing.
Annie I used to, when I was little. I was in a synogogue choir.
Robert So you're Jewish?
Annie No. But I like the music. I like the sound of Hebrew words. Sad sounds, sad songs. Lullabies in a language I don't understand, except for the sadness.
Robert Haunting.
Annie Yes.
Robert (*deep breath*) Your voice has haunted me for six months.

Annie Robert — you don't know me.

Robert But that's why.

Annie Why what?

Robert I *want* to know you. Annie, have dinner with me?

Annie Robert, I'm very flattered. But I'm very happy with David.

Robert Afternoon tea? Nursery sandwiches and Earl Grey?

Annie You're very sweet.

Robert Elevenses?

Annie Robert, what happened with Sarah?

Robert Sarah. I don't know really. Well, I do know. She just got tired. I was tired too. Bone tired. But I didn't know it until she asked me ——

Annie Asked you what?

Robert How I had the energy to keep trying. And I realized that I didn't.

Annie So you left?

Robert We both left. Without a trace.

Annie You forget that a relationship is two people, don't you? You get to think, after a while, that it's a *thing*. A kind of entity of its own, suspended between you.

Robert Like in art lessons, when you learn to paint the negative space before the objects. You start to think the space *is* an object.

Annie And then one person takes a step back, and you expect to hear it falling and crashing. But it doesn't 'cause there's nothing there. Except the other person.

Robert And if both people take a step back ——

Annie There's nothing there at all.

A pause

Robert Annie, I think we're very compatible.

Annie We don't *know* each other!

Robert Does Woody know you?

Annie David. And yes, he does.

Robert Maybe he just accepts you, without trying to understand you. Maybe you don't interest him very much.

Annie (*stung*) I'm going to hang up now, Robert. Thanks for calling. Have a nice day now. You've certainly made mine.

Robert Wait! Annie, Annie, wait! Please.

Annie Look, I know we seem to be in agreement here, but we've never talked about anything other than relationships. That doesn't mean we have anything in common. *Everyone* has relationships in common. And a mutual mistrust of relationships is no grounds for a relationship.

Robert We could try.

Annie Why would we *want* to?

Robert No, I mean, talking about something else. Come on. Think of a topic. Any topic. I'm open to suggestions.

Annie Robert, I wish I could help you. But I can't. You've dialled the wrong number again, Robert. I'm the wrong person.

Robert Allergies!

Annie What?

Robert Do you have any? I'm allergic to walnuts and that cheese with holes in.

Annie Emmenthal.

Robert And some brands of aftershave.

Annie I come out in a rash if I eat nuts.

Robert Walnuts?

Annie *All* nuts.

Robert (*triumphantly*) There you are, you see! I've never met anyone else who's allergic to walnuts. We're made for each other, Annie. We can anticipate a rosy old age together, helping each other avoid walnuts.

Annie I've managed quite well on my own so far.

Robert You're not on your own.

Annie No, but according to you David's bored senseless by me. He'd *encourage* me to eat walnuts.

Robert I didn't mean it like that. It came out wrong. He's fascinated by you. He must be.

Annie (*stiffly*) We are very happy at the moment.

Robert At the moment? You're so cynical.

Annie I can't afford not to be. Happiness is too good to last. It's a passing phase, like Rubik's cubes and pixie boots.

Robert I still have a Rubik's cube.

Annie Can you do it?

Robert I've never tried. I just take it to pieces and put it back together in the right order.

Annie Where's the challenge in that?

Robert Marry me.

Annie (*laughing*) I'm putting the phone down now, Robert. I'm putting it down because I have to, it's nearly two o'clock and I'm still in bed and I'm meeting David's sister in twenty minutes. And I'm putting it down because I want to. Not because I don't like talking to you. I do. But I love David, and I'm very happy, and I don't want to have an affair, or children, or afternoon tea with you.

Robert Elevenses, though?

Annie I hope something good happens for you, Robert.

Robert It's happened, Annie Hall.

Annie (*kindly*) Go away now, there's a dear.

Robert Goodbye Annie.

Annie Bye.

Annie replaces the receiver and stares at the telephone for a moment, smiling

Then she gets out of bed and walks offstage

Robert sits holding the phone

The Lights fade

SCENE 3

It is six months later. (This scene can be arranged by swapping Annie and Robert to each other's former side of the stage: Annie gets the kitchen, Robert the bedroom)

A bright, chilly Light floods the stage

Annie is in a different house. She sits at the kitchen table, which is littered with empty mugs, apple cores, ashtrays. She looks tired, and is scanning a newspaper without much interest. She wears a coat and scarf

Robert is sitting cross-legged on an unmade bed, holding the phone. On the floor is his ubiquitous packet of cornflakes, a packet of cigarettes, an empty bowl and a full ashtray. He dials and waits, humming softly

Annie's phone rings. She lets it ring a while before answering it

Annie Hallo.

Robert Annie Hall, I believe?

Annie Bloody hell! What did you do this time, contact a soothsayer?

Robert Almost. Your estate-agent. You moved in with Woody, right?

Annie Robert, I ——

Robert Wait, Annie. Don't worry. I'm not going to proposition you or propose to you, or make you share any kind of daytime snack with me.

Annie (*laughing*) Oh. Aren't you?

Robert I just wanted to tell you — something's happened.

Annie Don't tell me. You got your phone bill.

Robert I've met someone, Annie.

A pause

Annie Oh. That's — great. That's great, Robert.

Robert Her name's Moira and she's just — everything.

Annie How did you meet?

Robert In the queue for Lottery Tickets. We picked four out of six of the same numbers. 5, 11, 18 and 33. If that isn't fate, I don't know what it is.

Annie I think Camelot call it chance.

Robert Well I've never felt so lucky, Annie.

Annie (*warmly, moved*) You deserve it.

Robert We won twenty quid as well. Twenty quid each and a life-partner.

Annie Romantic.

Robert We bought champagne and chip-shop chips. I can't believe I'm this happy, Annie.

Annie I'm thrilled for you, Robert. Really. That's wonderful.

Robert You sound tired.

Annie I was up late.

Robert You were out. I tried to call last night.

Annie I was in. I was watching old episodes of *Falcon Crest* with the sound off.

Robert Annie, are you all right?

Annie No, Robert, I'm all wrong. But it's not forever. It's just a——

Robert Passing phase, like pixie boots.

Annie You have a kind of biannual memory system, don't you?

Robert I never forget you. I won't, ever.

Annie Well I think you should. Concentrate on Moira.

Robert I will. I do, I am. I intend to.

Annie Good.

Robert How's Woody?

Annie Oh, you know. Sunny in some places, dull in others.

Pause

Robert How would you like to go kite-flying?

Annie Oh Robert! You are in love with someone! Now stop this.

Robert I know. I just mean as friends. Not sexual kite-flying. Kite-flying as friends. That's all. I just want to meet you, just once. Look, you don't have to decide now. Just think about it. Take my number. You can call *me* next time, I always call you.

Annie Robert, dear ——

Robert Listen, Annie. I've asked Moira to marry me. We're engaged. We're getting married in July.

Annie That's terrific! Congratulations.

Robert So just meet me for a walk on the heath. Just as friends.
Like you meet Woody's sister.

Annie That was a one-off.

Robert This will be a one-off. Please. I'll never bother you again.
I'll disconnect my phone. I'll leave the country.

Annie (*smiling*) What's your number then?

Robert Oh, magic! Got a pen?

Annie I've got an eyeliner pencil.

Robert What will you use for your eyes?

Annie Biro, unless it's a special occasion.

Robert You're a funny girl, Annie.

Annie Tell me something I *don't* know.

Robert How about — 0171 701 8061.

She writes down the number

Got that?

Annie 0171 701 8061. Got it.

Robert Ring me. Anytime. Promise me.

Annie I promise.

Robert I have to go. I'm having lunch at Moira's. She *cooks*,
Annie. She cooks amazing things at lunchtimes. Even my Aunt
Sadie didn't do *lunchtimes*. You got a hardboiled egg in your
hand and a gingersnap if you'd been good. Moira does whole
dinners. I should dash or I'll be late. Don't forget to ring. Please
be OK. Goodbye Annie.

Annie Goodbye Robert.

Robert Bye.

Robert leaps up, combs his hair and puts on a jacket

*Annie sighs, and stands up, pulling a light suitcase from beneath
the table. She heads for the door*

*On impulse, both stop. Both look at their telephones. Annie returns
to the table slowly. She dials, and while she waits, she ignites the
piece of paper with her lighter and drops it into her ashtray*

Robert watches his phone. It rings. He picks it up

Robert Hallo?

Annie gently replaces her receiver. Robert smiles

Goodbye, Annie.

He puts down the phone, satisfied, and leaves the room

Annie shoulders her suitcase and does likewise

The piece of paper smoulders in the ashtray as the Lights go down to Black-out

FURNITURE AND PROPERTY LIST

Further dressing may be added at the director's discretion

SCENE 1

On stage: BEDROOM
Bed. *On it*: telephone, box of tissues, three empty cigarette packets, ashtray, nail file

KITCHEN
Kitchen table. *On it*: bowl of cornflakes, three empty cigarette packets, ashtray, telephone

SCENE 2

Strike: Box of tissues
Six empty cigarette packets
Nail file
Bowl of cornflakes

Set: BEDROOM
Novel
Two wine glasses
Empty wine bottle
Lighter
Cigarette

KITCHEN
Bowls
Mugs
Papers
Lighter
Cigarette

Personal: **Annie**: glasses

SCENE 3

Strike: Two wine glasses
           Empty bottle
           Novel
           Bowls
           Papers
           Bedroom lighter

Set: BEDROOM
           Packet of cornflakes
           Packet of cigarettes
           Empty bowl
           Full ashtray
           Comb

           KITCHEN
           Apple cores
           Ashtrays
           Newspaper
           Pen and paper
           Suitcase

LIGHTING PLOT

Practical fittings required: none
Interior. The same scene throughout

To open: Overall general lighting

Cue 1	**Robert** puts the phone down *Lights dim on the kitchen*	(Page 6)
Cue 2	**Annie** pauses, holding the phone *Lights dim on the bedroom*	(Page 6)
Cue 3	To open SCENE 2 Overall general lighting	(Page 7)
Cue 4	**Robert** sits holding the phone *Lights fade*	(Page 11)
Cue 5	To open SCENE 3 A bright, chilly light floods the stage	(Page 11)
Cue 6	**Annie** exits *Lights dim to black-out*	(Page 15)

EFFECTS PLOT

Printed by
THE KINGFISHER PRESS
London NW10 6UG